IT'S TIME TO EAT LIME

It's Time to Eat LIME

Walter the Educator

Silent King Books
A WhichHead Entertainment Imprint

Copyright © 2024 by Walter the Educator

All rights reserved. No part of this book may be reproduced in any manner whatsoever without written per- mission except in the case of brief quotations embodied in critical articles and reviews.

First Printing, 2024

Disclaimer

This book is a literary work; the story is not about specific persons, locations, situations, and/or circumstances unless mentioned in a historical context. Any resemblance to real persons, locations, situations, and/or circumstances is coincidental. This book is for entertainment and informational purposes only. The author and publisher offer this information without warranties expressed or implied. No matter the grounds, neither the author nor the publisher will be accountable for any losses, injuries, or other damages caused by the reader's use of this book. The use of this book acknowledges an understanding and acceptance of this disclaimer.

It's Time to Eat LIME is a collectible early learning book by Walter the Educator suitable for all ages belonging to Walter the Educator's Time to Eat Book Series. Collect more books at WaltertheEducator.com

USE THE EXTRA SPACE TO TAKE NOTES AND DOCUMENT YOUR MEMORIES

ns LIME

It's snack time now, what's on the way?

It's Time to Eat

Lime

A little green fruit to brighten your day!

Round and shiny, with a zesty glow,

It's time for lime, let's give it a go!

Take a lime and cut it in two,

Its scent is fresh, its color is true.

A tiny squeeze, the juice will flow,

Where does the limey magic go?

On tacos, salads, or fish so fine,

A splash of lime makes flavors shine.

It's tangy, tart, and oh-so-bright,

A little green fruit that feels just right.

Take a taste, so sour, oh my!

It makes you pucker and squint your eye.

But pair it with honey, sugar, or spice,

And suddenly lime is extra nice!

It's Time to Eat

Lime

Limeade's yummy, cool, and sweet,

A perfect drink for a summer treat.

Just squeeze your lime, add water and ice,

A sip of limeade feels so nice!

Did you know that limes love the sun?

They grow on trees 'til their job is done.

In warm, bright places, they soak up rays,

And ripen in the golden days.

Limes are healthy, packed with zest,

A boost of vitamins, they're the best!

They help you feel strong, they help you play,

A lime a day keeps the frowns away!

So next time you see this fruit so small,

Don't be afraid to give it your all.

Squeeze it, taste it, and share with a friend,

It's Time to Eat

Lime

The joy of lime will never end.

Lime on chips or squeezed on rice,

Lime in soup, it's always nice!

This little fruit is here to stay,

A zesty treat for any day.

Whether in a dish or on its own,

The lime brings magic all on its own.

A tiny fruit with so much cheer,

It's Time to Eat

Lime

It's time for lime, it's always near!

ABOUT THE CREATOR

Walter the Educator is one of the pseudonyms for Walter Anderson. Formally educated in Chemistry, Business, and Education, he is an educator, an author, a diverse entrepreneur, and he is the son of a disabled war veteran. "Walter the Educator" shares his time between educating and creating. He holds interests and owns several creative projects that entertain, enlighten, enhance, and educate, hoping to inspire and motivate you. Follow, find new works, and stay up to date with Walter the Educator™

at WaltertheEducator.com

www.ingramcontent.com/pod-product-compliance
Lightning Source LLC
LaVergne TN
LVHW010623070526
838199LV00063BA/5253